HARM

OMNIDAWN PUBLISHING   RICHMOND, CALIFORNIA

HILLARY GRAVENDYK

HARM

DESIGN AND COMPOSITION BY QUEMADURA

COVER PHOTOGRAPHS BY BENJAMIN BURRILL

PRINTED OFFSET ON ACID-FREE, RECYCLED PAPER

BY THOMSON-SHORE, INC., DEXTER, MICHIGAN

green press
INITIATIVE

Omnidawn Publishing is committed to preserving ancient forests and natural resources. We elected to print this title on 30% postconsumer recycled paper, processed chlorine-free. As a result, for this printing, we have saved:

2 Trees (40' tall and 6-8" diameter)
945 Gallons of Wastewater
1 million BTUs of Total Energy
60 Pounds of Solid Waste
210 Pounds of Greenhouse Gases

Omnidawn Publishing made this paper choice because our printer, Thomson-Shore, Inc., is a member of Green Press Initiative, a nonprofit program dedicated to supporting authors, publishers, and suppliers in their efforts to reduce their use of fiber obtained from endangered forests.

For more information, visit www.greenpressinitiative.org

Environmental impact estimates were made using the Environmental Defense Paper Calculator. For more information visit: www.edf.org/papercalculator

LIBRARY OF CONGRESS CATALOGING-IN-PUBLICATION DATA

GRAVENDYK, HILLARY, 1979–

HARM / HILLARY GRAVENDYK.

P. CM.

POEMS.

ISBN 978-1-890650-56-8 (PBK. : ALK. PAPER)

I. TITLE.

PS3607.R383H37 2011

811'.6–DC22

2011026841

PUBLISHED BY OMNIDAWN PUBLISHING

RICHMOND, CALIFORNIA WWW.OMNIDAWN.COM

[510] 237-5472 [800] 792-4957

10 9 8 7 6 5 4 3 2 1

FOR BENJAMIN

"Creature of occasion, remember where you have been, which leaves have teeth, which leaves are shaped like a pair of lungs." So begins "Botanica," the first poem in Hillary Gravendyk's singular lyric sequence. "The rocks chalked with mineral lines; the monstrous plant life. Imagine a carriage wheel turning on sand," she writes in the next "Botanica." Between responses that are perceived opposites—comfort or fear—a body finds its nature: *natura*, from *nasci*, "to be born" or, further in, from the root *gen?*, meaning, "to beget."

Harm is a collection of poems, some in short prose blocks, written in a great burst after the poet underwent major surgery. It is a cleanly and delicately paced volume, its pages sometimes punctuated by asterisks which suggest small flowers, snowflakes or abstract ink-breath. It is quiet, intense, and subtly beautiful work and, following in a long tradition in American poetry, is a book about both human and planetary illness, about the subjective experience of illness and the images that come to someone's consciousness in a time of illness. Thoughts about personal fate and of the present earth in peril are contiguous here. References to hospitals, to medical procedures and conditions are threaded with allusions to plants and to physical landscapes. Interiors trade place with exteriors; the meditating poet comes up for air in atmospheres that are literal and figurative. She transcends isolation and offers—not as palliative but as artistic practice—a sense of calm estrangement that often invokes an "other" in the work of a collective dream.

In fact, Gravendyk's book wrestles with several kinds of otherness in vocabularies that are by turns philosophical, psychological and ecologi-

cal. The style of the pieces is lyrical, occasionally disoriented yet familiar
—simultaneously surreal, Modernist and romantic. The fractured medi-
tations recall the work of Friedrich Hölderlin or René Char. In fact, read-
ing this work I was reminded of what Maurice Blanchot writes in his won-
derful essay on Char in *The Work of Fire*: "[The poem] is born before us and
in front of us, as our own future, as the unexpected that torments us and
fascinates us."

Gravendyk's poems also suggest the many senses of "the natural" as
they weave experiences of the world's body, the individual human body,
and the ephemeral body of the dream, inviting us to a palpable "other-
ness" that is here and not here, to physical existence and to the ineffable
existence that is always waiting to be experienced—just outside the im-
mediately familiar. She has done scholarly work on the poetry of Larry
Eigner, and while her aesthetic choices are mostly quite different from
his, Gravendyk puts forth her perceptions in quantum packets like
Eigner, phrase by phrase, and she writes toward a symbolic otherness.

The poet's lines often shuttle back and forth from isolated subjective
experiences of suffering to the hope for a redemptive dream-state; the
skeins are tangled and snagged. "Everything that measured measured
frantically." [untitled fragment]. The structures of her grammar shift—
sentences are sometimes conversational and sometimes oddly torqued.
In "Revisable Horizon," a complete sentence is placed between two sen-
tence fragments: "Spine like a string of little oceans. That's the back of
every you, the underside of the drain. Always stopped at some new brink."
The metaphor of the fluid spine or string offers surprise and fresh insight
as the spine evolves into a drain, and then to a horizon. The earth suffers;
things suffer as the body suffers.

Yet, despite urgent statements and emotionally wrenching material,
there is an even tone to this writing. Gravendyk's imagination is fertile,
and she is adept at following one image with another. Here is a fabric

metaphor in "Dark Alphabet": "But beloved error: a long braid of signs, given. Everyone is glowing with listening. Little syllabic string. Little tether. Line cast into a blacker sea." Her metaphors shift gently like those of Elizabeth Bishop, even though the halting procedures of her syntax sometimes channel Stein's music. The ontological gaze of the poet is occluded when simple distinctions fail ("That same music that terrifies / the mind, calms the blood") but is then clarified by the memory of a paradox, often in the form of an uneasy metaphor: "My body / humming like a hologram // struck from the air, / I picked up a brick // light as lava rock . . ." ["Anesthesia"].

An intuitive response to the mysterious process illuminated by the collection is to be found in one of lines near the end: "Language coils into each line" ["Secret Message"] The signs and signals ready themselves, and breath goes in and out of the body that is the world.

BRENDA HILLMAN / MAY 2011

HARM

Creature of occasion, remember where you have been, which leaves have teeth, which leaves are shaped like a pair of lungs. The closed landscape glitters. My name is *Acutifolius*: having sharp edges. Underside of each frond like a powdery line of Braille. Air stuttering with leaves. There's a night inside the night inside my chest. Forest air cool as a plum's dark flesh. The hand goes black against the low green. I'm *Candicans*: looking white or frosted. Or *Sylvaticus, Californicus*. In the crowded wood, I see the several eyes go down. Black air folds around low ferns. Asleep, I laid my hand on the tree until my skin turned to bark.

She left the body trailing its appetites

like a honeymoon. She left the body

permissionless, dreaming. A clot of institutional

mystics watched her slip the skin, gently shook

it from her shoulders. Stepping out of control

like riding a pinwheel. Everything was dazzling until

everything was dim. The light wilted across

the eyes. She left the body squandering

its machines. Mechanical eyes clicked open in the

lime-colored theatre. The closed air blushed

with cold. She hemmed a blanket of surrender,

cast it from herself. The body, an unlit

avenue of fireworks.

Quarter-light tips in.

A room shaped like a mismatched trio of brackets.

Each bend or angle bristling with other lights.

Drunken or weary. Lost or left.

In one bracket a chair. Dark monitor.

Disorder on a blacker field.

Someone's hands bound loosely down.

Skein of plastic braided into the mouth.

One hand charred black and almost

Black, a color like green. Wait—Mine.

Then I was lost in a stranger sound. Quarter-light tips out.

A machine gasps in surprise.

Throat closed by what opens inside it.

Mangy pressed minute hand, a scratch along the blank clock-face. Stalker moon.

In this all-night elaboration, all the language is the language of birds, damaging and certain.

It's not a bit like rest, these blown black hours. But now a darkening sea, now a white and rushing traffic, light combed into quick streaks.

Pink singing in the closed room, but actually, no one is sleeping, no one is getting out of bed.

You've unsealed each kissed brow, but when each turns to each, I'm out of range.

It's a careful violence but it executes a whole set of strangers, repeats, closer: That's the half-hour before I bloom in the eye of every you.

ASSESSMENT

Goes the day, bleached
of its figures:

The creature
of every failure,

skittering
across the road.

They found an error,
black with a white line,

and decided to have it
removed. A blank warren

folded behind every one
of their chests.

Goes the day and
the day's administration:

organs flat as mirrors,
the hour, a deflated body.

Grass in flat whorls show you bedding down in the wind. The rocks chalked with mineral lines; the monstrous plant life. Imagine a carriage wheel turning on sand. Crest of every rise on fire. The aspen flicking its wrist. I'm a line of apprentice observers, a field of insistent grass, seeds loosed from the stalk. Above the smoked glass of the sky, there's atmosphere. Underneath you, a cache of white shells. All the small scents close in the air: coyote mint, sage, dust. Softly, the dimmed hillside. I'm streaming away from you. The sound water makes when it runs through leaves.

Ahead the sky is winnowed to its smallest feature. Starred with damage, the body. What was promised, what was revealed. A long staircase of wounds. Behind: unseen error. Or accident. Harm winking on, a neon sign that says *closed*. Pain glued to each window. The rooms shadowed with harm. You offered anxiety, a harness made from care. Curved handle, intention. Harm a kind of adhesive. Skin clusters around the opening, ridged and thick. There are lighter and darker marks. They disclose. Paper echo, gesture. Bleakness along the spine of narrative. Harm flat as a swept floor. As a drawn planet. A bright story is requested. What will be touched? Machines, that flashing support, a threaded needle. And the body, sutured to harm.

Pain's absence, like a footprint in snow

but the iron had eaten into my flesh

there was nothing, nothing to record

*

*

Linen-thin scenes, stacked like records

my forest becomes a set of angles

a murmuring that betrays its worry

kaleidoscope panther on the black mountain

bright needle, punched through the neck

a hissing

someone brings in another chair

* ·

*

In the silent theatre, a confusion.

The blandness of the hour meets

The pink dreaming riot

*

*

The equivalence of dreams

To enter the room, you must "scrub in"

Shifting hillside, covered with crowns

Everyone bedded down in the playroom

*

*

Regret's silver string, binding the fingers together

That same music that terrifies

      the mind, calms the blood

Don't leave me

Don't leave the room.

*

*

How the sun turns over the body, returning

Light like a sweaty hand covering the face

Here, the atmosphere of a closed box

*

*

Ashy organ, breath of my breath

A blurry rope you throw me. Familiar. The color of air, doubled. The hand imprecise as a stilled wand. I surface. I submerge. The wink of meaning fleeing the scene. A letter clasped between the finger and the eye. We add them up and they equal troubling dreams. Worry buried in the folds. Extended across a simple language, there is a confusion of longing. Technicolor handprint, clasping at need. Absent clarity, I waver in the harsh light. But beloved error: a long braid of signs, given. Everyone is glowing with listening. Little syllabic string. Little tether. Line cast into a blacker sea.

*

Someone whistled

across a crumbling bridge

sweetened with snow,

the place where I fall

into a clear sound.

Cried out as feeling rushed

along the coal lining.

Little tantrum lifted

by degrees—

DEPTH SOUNDING

Hand me the vanishing alphabet or

read me something practical:

the brain records for once what

looks like wakefulness.

In the throat, a rising panic

sour, steady as an intravenous stream

of dandelions.

With one hand I telephoned

the roofline for a row of pigeons.

The pupil a smooth black pill.

Give me the sound of waking:

the hiss and shush of machines flickering on.

Scratch across the eyelid like a penciled alley

intricately branched,

seldom traveled.

The route within is familiar—
dedicated pilgrims

prefer circuits, only sentiment
dictates a frontier.

So there is a way-chapel
of cell gray stars, there
a nucleus of wet pebbles,
laid in moss—

twigs crossed in an arrow
intently, absently
must, after all, mark.

Your hand is a furrow pressing
out a darkness and in the stuttering
breath, a portal—

Nimbus cloud lung
shuddering toward the gash
of morning, remember:

pioneers slash only toward a territory
they remember.

The vein is an intimate thoroughfare.
Still, nothing comes first.

The heart expands in circles:
the pioneer,
the pilgrim,
both gather at the core—

one tearing out the bright veins,
one tending their short light.

*

How we are meant to recall our disappearances:

worry braided into the softest cage

what we've never remembered

pressed into skin.

Spine like a string of little oceans. That's the back of every you, the under-side of the drain. Always stopped at some new brink. There was certainty and there was anxiety, ringing sharply in the head. In a crowd of animals pursuing each other, I was a ring of blue gas. Hushed into my own heat. There were onlookers. The problem of suffering as a set of values is the way a feather crumples at the edge of any flame. Cringing into itself. How hard to play to that smallest audience, where it's just your own eyes tun-neling to your own chest. After a while, that tidal motion. Something washes in, covering. No revisable horizon. But a cord of carved symbols, rising to the hand.

Thicket of tall signs and a leafy coolness. Footstep like a crumpled page. It isn't prowling, it's the secret of animals. Eye to the green air. Footstep like a bone snapping. The kind of hunger that swallows you. A scene-stealing cast of birds. Something nestled, nestling. Footstep like a mouse-trap. All the smaller creatures a glassy glitter along the floor. The collec-tive appetite of bees. Belly sown with stone. Footstep like a wind tunnel. A punishment of dogs, a grief of snakes. White promise dull on the tongue. What is kept, what is exchanged. Run or water, basket or bomb. A sharp gift for another. What big woods these are. Who goes softly there? Footstep like a fire blooming. Mouth: my heart, opening wide.

As to the sleeping tree hollowed out

in the woods: it fell, deeply, into a notched boat.

Waveless forest floor, shadowed heart, stand of ironwood.

In the meantime. In some time. A bunker in readiness for a flood.

Boat unlifted. Unmet sea. Needful body, uncarried.

As to the dreaming craft lightened by journeys:

it was a swiftly parted school of lime-bright fish.

I was nameless. Delivered.

Solitude, my own invention.

Spun sky, unhappy stairway. Stark record of summer: bright, harrowing. But it wasn't the brink. It was an uneven surface, was a jumble of absences. They waited for me in the sycamore shade. Violet current, stuttering eye. Watching me disappear by degrees. You pressed my shoulder, held it to the wheel. And I haven't even told you what I fear most, what's buried in the flesh. Selfish desire, I kept you like a secret. Wanted what I could get. We built a boat from all this, set it adrift in the tarpaper night. Mended my skin with barbed-wire. Covered ourselves in refusal. I forced your hand into mine, though I knew you couldn't go where I had to go.

bundle of fat roads that prop the lips apart

chin like a storm drain, always flooded

rural route across the cheek and

underground two glittering machines exhale slowly

one fluttering its ragged paper flags

the other a metal pulley that hoists and lowers them—

and then the body: surrendering again and again

You asked every question in order, waited
for me to blink *yes*. I handed over a new
wound, they wound machines into my skin,
made a circle of lights in my field of vision.
Someone came a long way. Bandaged
my hand in leaves, bruised my hair. Pushed
me from side to side like a cradle. There were
unquiet threats in the corridor. It was a scarred
mountain, busy with trees.
Or a busy wing, feathered with records. You
closed your mouth and wondered, pressed
a penny into the palm. Pinned
supposition to the cork wall, still fluttering.
Time was stupid and I was bursting
with alphabets to tender. To keep. We
were all noiseless, all unready.

We move toward the insignificant

sea, the one

at the lip of every cliff—

if you'd speak of it

you'd say I'm like a cloud

of ash

you can move

right through

*

You were the Librarian
of caution, the most
unwelcome ghost.

Tiny book, tiny book
keeper. You have always
been accounted for.

Stitches in the dirt make a suggestion, legible, piled on one side. Pebble-fist path, whiskertree, stun, little sunclot.

The fullness of the account. Teaspoon spade to take measure. A largesse of ritual. Archeology of remainders. Clay, cedarhair, rock, rock, peat.

Whose shard arranged into hours. Curt sacrifice. Spinning sodwheel, start and stop. With clues. Little foot-pedal of ground.

Made a packet of crushed cement, ghost orchard & firepit. Little buried stairway. Little burial. Clock of clean bones burned white.

To know me as golden is to know me all wrong. Every time I breathe in it
   smells rusty, like blood, and when I cough there is blood in the air.

If I were in charge of these special effects, I'd make it thicker; it's so hard
   to take it seriously. Bright little hearts and stars and carnations on a
   white cloth.

Let's go out with a thicker line, a cerulean skylight, rain that gets dumped
   out of a trough to thwack the pane of glass, a smear of red like tempera
   paint across the cheek or the hand, streaming from the mouth.

Let's have a disaster, a lake made of salt, a blackout. Everything riots and
   unspools, the whole room on one side and all the sound winking out.

You stay here. Let me run into that starring role, pinker and more flooded
   with blood: remember when it meant exuberance, remember awe?
   Let's be that breathless.

Soil breathes its own warning: spores of *aspergillus* loosed in the air, sucked in. Raised black patches on the fingertip and the back of the hand. That gropes in loam, that covers its own heart. Dirt like a bandage across the chest. Charred hand, disappearing at the edges. At the sight of my own body, I turn cold. Light at the seams. Hard to believe you must bury some things to bring them to life. The bed bridles with its spiny markers, all labeled *sleep*. Pricked with reminders. The light speckled like an egg. There are several common names for precaution: one is *superstition*, one is *omission*. But what protections unravel an older harm?

I was promised only good things. Basket filled with honey or the equiva-
lent of honey. A thicket of long pines rimming the strayable path. Animals
rustling. Had a cloak but left my head bare. Warning left its signature.
Whiter horizon, a splinter. Basket of clever birds. Crossed the threshold of
every afternoon at once. You were a series of obvious errors. A room close
as the inside of a mouth, a basket packed with nettles. Costumed heart.
I made a delivery; you were made of appetites. Timberwood, tinder. So I
waited in the slick sack of your belly. Flinched when the axe came through.
Shed you like a wet coat.

ANESTHESIA

Prepped by strangers, I
counted backwards

into a storm,
the eye shuttered against

the tumult, the mouth
slapped open by rain.

Heard a plucked sound
circling itself

chirrup of mechanized insects
their practical violence

saved for me. My body
humming like a hologram

struck from the air,
I picked up a brick

light as lava rock and, blurred
with dreaming, the eye fell

over a book of impossible acts
completing themselves.

A hot room where nothing was wasted. I ate what had been relayed. Can't have said more than *take care*. Everyone under the same spell. A fervent goodness, a melancholy leave-taking. After all there was darkness before there were shards of mirror. Enchanted. The cold queen makes a brief appearance. Robe of furred snow. Someone unlocks the cracked-ice lake. Hands black with cold. Someone plucks the nugget of glass from the eye. Or it is a reflection. Or it was made of ice. Or it was forgotten.

Nested rooms, cocoon of every embarrassment.

Lifted up, laid down. The octagonal hallway

branching against the walls. A rail, ridden.

Cluster of women leaned over a monitor.

They clap at the first lap. Dark breath

pulled behind the eyes and the teeth.

The doorways shiver or spin: the eye

cannot be trusted, cannot rest. In the morning

I sit up straight, ask for approval. Later

they'll bind me with protective measures.

Exposure at the edges. Who knew such things

could be forgotten? There is a hesitation before

every response. Limbs filled with sand.

Someone waits ahead, posing new difficulties.

Offering the crook of an arm, everyone slows

their pace. Everyone wears patience like a coat.

Walking like a kind of waiting.

Handful of explosions down the mouth's hatch. We've followed unlikely directions. Orange octagon, clear green cap. There isn't a favorite time of day, there are daily performances. Walk along the contaminated street. White disc, pink lozenge. Let's steal precaution. Ask me what I'd like to buy, if I've been to Mexico. Hand over the glossary of hesitation, the one where the entry for every word is blank. Needle, circle. It isn't actually a story, it's more like a kind of sleep you keep falling into. A kind you keep close.

Mute lake, cold at the lip
where sound throbs,
milk-white,
across patterned moss

hard knot of honey
stays the tongue
in a room of invented gods
thatched with insects.

These were our secrets: samples from a charred heart, beak ligament, sharp fist of serpentine. We traded our phosphorous and filament for a ten-pin lock and were comforted. We knew that the right chemicals could make anything glow, knew that our discoveries were too delicate for exposure, and how distant, how troubling outside our rare cabinets! A little more protection and another specimen: clinging ring of iris, breath-bottle, bone, or scab. It was dangerous but it was ours for safekeeping. We wanted something coarser than blood to course through us: beeswarm and fiberglass. Wanted to glitter and wound at the same time.

Now in the lidded field a bird

skids—bursts across a sense

burdened with expectation

facing out.

Husks slippery

with sameness,

another repetition

taped to the back of the eye.

Find tinctures for boldness,

or blacken a knuckle with charred

tree, or sleep outside a fogbank,

blurred with silica. Don't answer

the sound of the tightened sun

or our creatures, hollering and

musky with harm.

It's the shape of things dearly meant: a card of buttons, pressed in. White-ish hour. Burden, fledgling. A new kind of lightbulb. Whatever we were promised; whatever we'd done. Starker logic. The age of glaciers, of celibacy. Meteorite. Comma shoreline; comma sun. Big and little ocean. Sediment ring. Darling raincloud, constellation, harm. Grief was one technique. Also burrow, also foxhole. Tempest, cycle, also doubt. Buried what we had, but above us.

You packed a suitcase
with bees, collected honey
in the lining. The window

open like a palm. You thought
you knew what you were getting
into. Circumstantial organs and my voice

splitting in two. I felt sorry
for love. I felt sorry.
Every exchange was letter-pressed

on my skin. Then someone made ornaments
of affect. They were charms against
protection.

We asked for direction: Which catacombs
exit to the street? Strangers pointed
at every door.

The building in the shape
of a jaw. Your certainty.
Your domino heart.

You lined your pockets
with bees you shoved your hand
right in.

*

There is a break under the skin,

forced up like a rough stone.

Someone threaded a loom

of nails, spelled *gentle ghost.*

What haunts us is our softness

When we touch the places our chests are closed

against each other.

LOVE POEM

You were a blade
bent for the narrow slip
into a bladed paleness
into the rushing down which
is the place that softness goes
when it goes—

Or you were the sheath
slung above the scuttled water.
And for a minute you were the signal,
the stop, the start, you
your taut suicide arch,
you, your arrow, your bow—

Just as fish hurdle into air
and are stricken with what is raw
and empty, after all, about air:
you stayed the seam between
poise and plunge, the line from which
every letter is pressed.

Shore curved like an instep against the soft fray of water
but all the litter of other lives
and minus shells, minus salt glass.
Busted bronze chandelier and peg-legged sofa
little clutch of crabs that scroll across
the Monopoly board, one claw waving a house
too small to inhabit. In a minute the ocean settles
over it all, like a thin shift, covering slight and clinging,
showing off a coat rack's decorative nipples
and the thatch of russet feathers
from a stuffed sparrow breast. When it rolls
out again there is one line less.
We read the scene and it says
opportunity but after a while it also says
obligation and my love says *only watch.*

Ankle-deep in brackish bric-a-brac
I'm still filling my pockets
and stashing boxes above the water line
frenzied, though we are so far from home
on the curved beach held tight by cliffs.
It could be an island,
it could be the island of lost things,
could be how we are meant to lose them
when they wash up for a brief time
irresistibly arrayed—

I wanted to show you the butterscotch bark
of the pine. The ten tiny portraits in the blossom's

eye, the licorice ridgeline, the way
the traffic light repeats itself. How

I wanted to find you insects backlit in trees, the fourth
color only birds see. Wanted to walk with you toward

the season's last snowfield, show you the radio's
private life. What, after all, did I show you?

only how the body betrays every
impulse, gathers every name to itself.

We sat on the reluctant
roof, watching miniature neighbors
set fire to each other.

A warm wind on our
foreheads. Cherry bomb
weather.

I held the heat in my hand
like an apple—

leaving has
a temperature, a
pressure.

Appetite, a front
moving in.

Hived lung, yellow and tangled with blue air. At the office of synchro-
nized bowers, she charges up the dirt stair and vanishes into the promis-
ing veil of brightness. Reflection studded sky, greening and pitted with
green weeds; the green-eyed hills carved into an unburnt hearth, purple
with cold. She wanders in gladness, picks along the rinsed-rock ridge,
curls into the heat of bleached summit, the blood warming in its tunnels,
the ice cracking underfoot. Now she emerges from the breath-hot cloud,
perhaps, into sharp air thinned like a row of seedlings. Passes beneath the
stiff wing of a white fir, or beneath the shadowed ripple of a bird, flinch-
ing in the skeletal air. Once I whitened the hides of animals with a blue
soap, a prism trick. Once the crowded cattle pressed their hooves into
the purple-black muck, and slept dreamless and musky with each others
heat. In the slippery grooves of the chest another sleep ratchets closer, yel-
low with significance, clouded with ash.

YOU WERE THERE

was foraging outside a patch of burning birds,
papering and evaporated blue over a thin field

and caught myself inside a nest like an eroded cliff
or the strutted gap between vent and vented, formally

and humming or I was the wing and circle saw
full of hungry throats or bound to them and fleeing

or trees pierced into a scatter of trajectory, or cars
torched and chiming, and/or you were there:

carrier cloud, you empty along the bottled breakers,
you the jealousy harp, you the scenting water, and

you the lakeward, the forget,
you the clapper of each bell.

REJECTION

Glass needle bright
as a small sun, set down.

The body's protections make
something to fear.

Honeycomb lung you
were whiter then,

your light-box heart, lit
for every occasion.

In these plain rooms, in a language
that separates us

you refuse me.

They'll map this secret
body, the one shiny with blood.

Small airways cast in
collagen's net. And wired

behind the sternum:
instinct's animal.

Scarred stranger,
you go by degrees:

one moment, then another
left to other devices.

Familiar walk, embellished with breath.

Circle, incline, field of visions. I wasn't

expecting you so soon. At night, you are a sky-colored

stone obscured by the skin around you. Familiar heft,

embellished with breath.

In my house there is a staircase with a thousand

steps. Blurry spiral, spinning forehead. You are

that hissing noise memorized in sleep. Familiar

sound, embellished with breath.

I'll decorate each hour with willful ignorance,

with refusal. Cluster of dim signals that

spell out *slowly*. Curvature of the sun, blanket moon.

They wink on at irregular intervals. Familiar sky, embellished with breath. My intimate, my familiar: I thought

you would follow, quietly. A sound where

no sound should be. But there is no now—

only breath, threading its tiny needles.

I think I thought I'd never have to lift the body across the room again. Thought it could be replaced. Hands plunging into that mess of organs and blood, grafting an other to the windpipe, to the underside of the heart. What is it that's been left behind? Now a Ziploc ribcage, sealed against some other harm. The kind of awe you hide from. It stretches from one armpit to the other, softens under each breast, thickens at the clavicle into a perforated ridge. That tender barrier—breached, so we call it cure. But there is none, only different kinds of wonder. Now an engraved avenue stretches across the chest; islands spangle the belly. Call me cyborg, call me monster, miracle. Read the line of my flesh aloud and I'll listen.

*

There is a pixilation along
the seam, the prints of
our tiniest creatures.

You saved every staple in a plastic cup
each suture a deserted bridge
displaced from that softness.

We've turned down the corners of facing pages. Some picture the patch-
work brain. Others feature just the sound of it, cycling through rele-
vant quadrants: Blue, red, green, left, red, yellow.

We've turned down the same aisles before, seeking elaborater grammars.
Here where we used to separate novels from rabbit thickets, from
sealed-off street scenes. Where a carnival of spines lit up at sundown,
wheeling.

I wrote you a letter in my sleep. Your eyes were the folded corners. My
breath made a grey smudge across your cheek, as if it were a thumb,
as if I had been reading the news. We fell into separate versions of
the same dream, then away.

We've turned down one alphabet after another. As if we could bind in
both directions and leave an open passage. As if we could read with-
out it. Commonly. But we've invented an apparatus to solve this
problem: it blows out every candle at once.

*

When you came to me, fog drawn across your faces,

Everything that measured measured frantically.

You said my eyes were like guttering suns

I flickered in and out of range—

Thread of tiny pulses, the breath, beating.
Ask me if I can walk through the boarding gate.
The plastic leash clear with effort, that's mine.

The last time this way, or simply the last time.
You promised me a burden, a heartsleeve—
the answer is *yes*, but wears its caveats like a bracelet.

Little hive buried in the chest, little swarm
I know perfectly well what you mean.
Every telephone call a fishhook in the spine.

Gemstone blood if we wait quietly
cornered in this ferocious *cul-de-sac*.
Darling harm, an arrow in the only direction.

I shed the animals of care each evening
when there's nowhere to go but inside the well—
there, where it's always cool, always grave.

Corona of uncertainty, the crown of every hour
it's a flatness that tightens the skin,
you wear it with me for the last time.

O sweet pretender, tell me it's now I'm afraid of:
this gasping in the bright sun
with darkness on the sun's far side.

Fell through the alphabet then
it darkened like a pane of glass
I'd stare blankly
through

if each sign revives a pinprick
of awareness

if there is nothing left to say but
come back

Still, language coils into each line
I cling to

Fell through the bright sound
of voices offering me solace saw
the beacon letterboard star of waking—
wondered

what
signal do I give
when I give way?

Woke up from one dream and into another.

I guess I'd written *time was honey*. Wrote myself a landscape. Slow scenery,
   combed gold across the mouth and the eye.

But our fast-forwarding hearts. Every eye the thawed river, fat with snow.

Mind rode in the back of a train out of one weather and into another.

Then cool down the well of an old attachment. Folded my arms and my
   legs up like a scarab.

The sound was blue metal, stiff and clicking.

Chose the food, but the tables were full of strangers. Sluggish and
   satisfied conversation I couldn't ignore, couldn't stand.

I'll impose a narrative across an abrupt jumble of absences, call it *healing*.
   But each blank moment departs us, too.

Lost the book of what happens next—and anyway, closed, one book looks
   so like another.

*

NOTES

The first italicized line in "The Seven Sins of Memory" was drawn from Mary Shelley's *Frankenstein: or, the Modern Prometheus*.

The first line of "Exuberance" is an altered version of a line from the Band of Horses song, "Funeral."

"Gentle ghost," referenced in one of the untitled fragments, refers to a miniature art installation at Vermont Studio Center.

"Beneath the Stiff Wing of a White Fir" borrows from and responds to Samuel Taylor Coleridge's "This Lime-tree Bower my Prison."

ACKNOWLEDGMENTS

Special thanks must be given to a few people who, at various stages,
edited and championed these poems. This book would not have
been the same without the essential aid of Brenda Hillman.
Margaret Ronda and Jessica Fisher also provided encouragement
and editorial help. The first poems for this book were drafted
with the help of my Jeffrey House housemates at Squaw Valley.

Thanks, also, to Rusty Morrison and Ken Keegan at Omnidawn,
who made publishing a lovely experience for this author. Many
thanks to Jeff Clark at Quemadura, who made this book beautiful.

I am grateful to my sister, Megan Gravendyk, who is my
writing partner and sounding board and who wrote
alongside me during many crucial moments.

Love and thanks to my parents, John and Katherine Gravendyk,
who bought me a little green desk when I was two years old.
Their encouragement has shaped my work.

I'd also like to thank the editors at *Tarpaulin Sky, Octopus*, and
The Bellingham Review where some of these poems first appeared in
slightly altered forms. Jane Miller chose "Exuberance" and "Night
Wing" as winners of the 2011 *Lana Turner* Open Poetry Contest.

This book owes itself, in a large part, to the love, good humor,
keen ear, and unwavering support of my husband, 7.
Thank you, Benjamin; this book is for you.

Hillary Gravendyk is an Assistant Professor of English at Pomona College in Claremont, California. She received her PhD in English from the University of California, Berkeley. Her chapbook, *The Naturalist*, was published by Achiote Press in 2008. She lives on the eastern edge of Los Angeles county.